A Curious Explorer's Play-Quest

Adult Facilitator Guide

Your World. Your Way.

Picture It. Choose It.
Focus on It. Create It.

Demetra Yuvanu

Ages 8-12

Copyright © 2025 Demetra Yuvanu

All rights reserved. No part of this publication may be reproduced stored in a retrieval system, or transmitted, in any form or by any means, electronic, mechanical photocopying, recording, or otherwise, without the written prior permission of the author.

Illustrations by Creative Florence
www.creativeflorence.uk

ISBN 978-0-9840421-6-6

Demanu Books LLC
November 2025

This book uses the Dyslexie font
the typeface for people with dyslexia.
www.dyslexiefont.com

Table of Contents

1. Welcome to the Mystery Behind the Doors Companion Guide
2. Child Play-Quest Experience
3. Why Your Presence Matters
4. How to Use This Play-Quest
5. Before You Begin This Play-Quest
6. The Three Magical Doors: An Overview for Adults
7. Nurturing Choice and Focus in Door Three
8. Helping Children Understand Their Power
9. Bringing Choice and Focus into Everyday Life
10. Quick Reminders for Grown-Ups
11. Your Own Reflections
12. Recapping
13. Epilogue and Next Steps

1
Welcome to the Mystery Behind the Doors Companion Guide

This guide is for you, the adult who's walking alongside a child.

It's distilled from my own experiences and the lessons I've learned along the way, as both a mother and a grandmother of two. I have been enriched by my roots in Europe, and the diverse experiences I've had in Turkey, and several USA states.

My hope is to share what's worked for me, so that kids can benefit by Gaining tools that help them navigate life with confidence and joy. To stand tall, make empowered choices, and unlock their full potential from the start.

In this Play-Quest, your child will step through each door for a brief preview, offering not just a reminder but a reinforcement of the timeless truths they discovered in *Mystery Behind the Doors.* They'll have the opportunity to actively work with these truths, applying them to their own lives through hands-on exercises.

Whether you're a parent, teacher, or caregiver, your role isn't to teach or fix. It's to offer presence, attention, and a little structure as your child explores the powerful ideas of focus, emotion, and choice.

This experience is designed to be creative and intuitive, not rigid or restrictive. Let's explore the first timeless truth, the power of focus: *"When we focus on something, we have the power to transform not just how we feel, but what we do."*

Example: Imagine you're learning to build a **LEGO** tower. If you keep noticing how it keeps falling, you'll feel frustrated and that will make your progress more challenging. However, if you focus on your own strengths and persistence, you'll harness the power of transformation and ultimately achieve better results.

2
Child Play-Quest Experience

To start the Play-Quest experience, you'll find that this adult guide is just one half of the journey; the other half is a simple, open-ended Play-Quest where your child can explore these ideas in their own way. Instead of just reviewing concepts, they'll have a chance to make these lessons part of their everyday life. Together, you'll find this process both enriching and enjoyable.

As you guide your child through this workshop, you can encourage them to break big challenges into smaller, manageable pieces. You can gently suggest that they think about transforming something they find difficult into smaller steps.

You have two ways to access the child's Play-Quest:

1. Download and print it using the free link or **QR** code in the back of this guide.

This way, each child can have their own copy, while you keep this guide as your reference.

2. **Or** purchase the printed version on Amazon.

3
Why Your Presence Matters

In this Play-Quest, the same ageless truth you were introduced to in the book *Mystery Behind the Doors* — what we focus on expands — is put into action. But here, it's not only used for achieving goals; it's also about helping shift moods and perspectives.

If a situation feels tough or gloomy, we can guide children to gently shift their thoughts and find a brighter angle. And it's okay if that means sometimes shifting their thoughts and sometimes stepping away for a moment.

Both of these approaches help

them learn how to choose their perspective, and see the results of that shift.

As they see and practice how this works, it's crucial that they also have a safe space where they are genuinely seen and heard.

This Play-Quest isn't just about helping them understand the book. It's about helping them understand themselves.

When you sit beside them, ask gentle questions, or simply offer the time and space for exploration, while you're sending the message:
"What you feel and notice matters and expands."

You don't need to interpret their drawings or lead them toward answers. You just need to be there, open, interested, and supportive.

That's more powerful than any script.

How to Use This Play-Quest

This guidebook gives you everything you need to guide the experience. Inside, you'll find insights into the three doors, along with reflection prompts, gentle language, and suggestions on how to bring the message to life in everyday ways.

One effective way to offer the Play-Quest is to break it down into weekly segments.

Perhaps aiming for about six weeks with roughly two chapters per week. But feel free to adjust the pace based on your child's needs. Each session can take about one to one and a half hours to complete, allowing plenty of time for writing, drawing, and reflection.

With this steady pace, children can absorb each timeless truth and apply it effectively.

What You'll Need:
- This guidebook
- Access to the child's Play-Quest—printed or as a free PDF.
- Blank paper, if you prefer not to write in the printed book.

To get started, take time to look through this adult guide yourself. No rush. No pressure.

As you guide your child through this journey, remember to encourage curiosity and celebrate progress.

Take time to reflect on the experiences together, discussing what you've both learned along the way.

5
Before You Begin the Play-Quest

Before inviting your child into this experience, take a moment for yourself. This isn't just an activity for them; it's a shared journey. The more grounded and open you are, the more magical the quest becomes.
You might want to ask yourself:
- "What do I want to bring into this time together?"
- "What kind of energy or mood would I like to set?"
- "Am I willing to be surprised?"

You don't need to have all the answers. Just show up.

And remember, this Play-Quest

isn't about performance, it's about connection. Some parts may feel light and silly, while others might come across as more thoughtful or meaningful. All of it is welcome.

Your job isn't to teach—it's to walk alongside. Now, you're ready to open the doors.

6

The Three Magical Doors: An Overview for Adults

In this chapter, you will discover how to support your child through each magical door, each leading them into a unique enchanted land.

Each door represents a different theme that shows children the power of focus, the freedom of choice, and the importance of action in transformation.

As you journey beside your child, I encourage you to share your own experiences of choosing to focus on the positive, and how that choice brought more calm or beauty into your life.

When children step through the

first door, into the Land of Beauty, they enter a vibrant, colorful land filled with beautiful flowers, singing birds, and delightful aromas. The more they focus on and appreciate the beauty around them, the more vibrant and enchanting the land becomes.

This teaches children that focusing on the positive and beautiful aspects of life brings even more positivity and beauty into their experience.

Stepping through the second door into the Land of "Yuck", children encounter a dull and dreary environment. The lesson here is that when they focus on the negative aspects, like the mud or the lack of color, those aspects too grow and become more prominent.

This teaches children about the

power of their focus and attention. That the end result is just the same, whether focusing on the positive or the negative.

Finally, when they step through the third door, they find themselves in the mystical Land of Choice. This enchanted land is split into two distinct sides, one vibrant and beautiful like the first land, and the other dull and muddy like the second. At this point, children notice how their focus influences their experience, and as they explore they notice how their attention shapes the world around them. If they focus on the bright side, that side expands. If they linger on the dreary side, it begins to take over.

This land is where the core message of *Mystery Behind the Doors*, the middle grade novel, comes to life: "*We have the power to choose what we focus on and that choice shapes our experience.*"

For adults, this entire journey offers a powerful way to let children learn through their own play, without the need to preach.

By encouraging them to reflect and express their experiences through words and drawings, you help them understand these concepts more deeply.

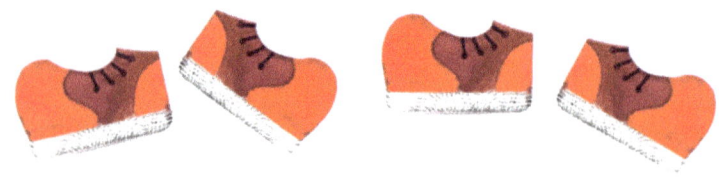

7
Nurturing Choice and Focus in Door Three

Let's take a closer look at what happens when a child enters the third door.

This land invites children to notice their own ability to choose. It encourages gentle awareness rather than quick answers. It helps build trust in their own feelings and sense of worth.

It also helps children witness the magic of their own curiosity, attention and imagination.

As guides in this Play-Quest, adults can help children understand the importance of making intentional decisions.

Through consistent, mindful choices, mastery can be achieved.

In *Mystery Behind the Doors*, Haris decided to change his inner dialogue. Armed with his new mindset, he approached his challenge with intention and focus. Each practice became an act of choice—steady, mindful and full of purpose. His persistence paid off, and he not only succeeded, but also realized that he had the ability to choose how to meet every challenge with confidence.

8
Helping Children Understand Their Power

After guiding children through door three, encourage them to reflect on their own choices, their impact, and articulate those reflections in their own words.

Resist the urge to explain too much—this is where their own inner discoveries matter most. Your role is to stay curious and supportive.

Some children might intuitively link their focus with their emotions. For example, you might notice your child realizing that when focusing on something beautiful, it makes him or her calmer and happier.

Others might say that they feel

restless when they focus on something that does not inspire them. The key is to support their unique feelings and plant a seed without forcing insight.

Over time, these ideas will naturally take root, especially if you revisit them gently through stories, conversations, or choices in daily life.

Here is a prompt you can use:

"I wonder what you noticed in your imagination and what feelings you had when you made your choice?"

Bringing Focus and Choice into Everyday Life

The magic of the three doors doesn't end when the Play-Quest is over. In fact, this is where it begins to live and breathe in your child's world.

As an adult, you have the chance to gently reinforce what your child experienced—without turning it into a lecture. The idea is to notice small moments and reflect them back, almost like holding up a mirror.

For example, when a child gets stuck in a complaint or frustration, you might say:

"Hmm... sounds like we might be standing on the gloomy side of the Land of Choice right now. Want to

see if we can take a step toward the bright side?"

Or when they shift their attitude and brighten up:

"Wow, did you feel that? I think you just changed the whole landscape—just like in the Land of Choice."

Over time, these small nods help them build self-awareness and a sense of agency. They begin to understand that they are active participants in their own experience.

And remember, it works both ways.

If you find yourself stuck in a draining moment, you can pause and say aloud: *"I think I've been staring at the muddy side. I'm going to look at the beautiful side now."*

Let them see you use the same transformative tools they've been playing with.

10

Quick Reminders for Grown-Ups

- Let the child lead. Trust their perception—even if they don't use the words you expect.
- Stay curious. Ask open-ended questions like: *"What did you notice?"* instead of jumping in with explanations.
- Use playful language. Refer back to the magical lands when things get tough or stuck.
- Model the message. Let your child see you shift your focus, too—it teaches more than words ever could.

- Keep it light. This is not about fixing or correcting—it's about planting seeds of awareness through joy and curiosity.

11
Your Own Reflections

Let's take a moment to sit quietly and think about what happened in the Land of Choice.

After the children have drawn or described their own experiences, you can then reflect on your own perspective.

Which side did you find yourself focusing on more—the bright side or the dreary one? How did it feel when you focused on each side?

Have you ever noticed that when you focus on something that makes you happy or proud, more good feelings seem to come?

And when you think a lot about

something that bothers you, it feels like it takes over?

You have a special power—your choice of focus.

12
Recapping

You've walked through the three doors, reflected on their meaning, and considered how to guide your child with care and presence.

Now it's time to wrap things up. No need for a big setup. Let them explore, create, and reflect in their own way. Trust that the seeds you've planted will grow—in quiet moments, in small shifts, and in the way they begin to see the world around them. Whether you sit beside them, check in afterward, or give them space to explore on their own, your presence has already made a difference. You've set the tone and opened the doors.

The rest belongs to your child.
This guide is complete.

13
Epilogue and Next Steps

If you haven't already downloaded the child's Play-Quest, you can do so by visiting the link below or scanning the QR code.

This adult guide is one half of the experience. It's the child's Play-Quest that completes the journey.

Remember, the real magic unfolds as you and your young explorer, or even a whole group of curious adventurers, dive into the world of *Mystery Behind the Doors.*

I hope these next steps bring joy and new discoveries, whether at home or in a classroom full of eager minds.

May these timeless truths, which form the very foundation of transformation and creation, come to life through this Play-Quest and serve as a bridge connecting them to your shared life journey.

Remember, it's both your adventure and your child's. As you guide them, your own perspective will evolve, strengthening the bond between you.

Through these timeless truths, you'll both discover new ways to connect and thrive together.

https://bit.ly/CuriousExplorerPlayQuest

Keep Questioning.

Keep Evolving.

Keep Noticing.

Their Future.
Your Wisdom.
Your Way.

www.ingramcontent.com/pod-product-compliance
Lightning Source LLC
Chambersburg PA
CBHW062106290426
44110CB00022B/2734